A Bank Robber's End

The Death of Jesse James

Ryan Randolph

rosen central
Primary Source™

The Rosen Publishing Group, Inc., New York

Published in 2004 by The Rosen Publishing Group, Inc.
29 East 21st Street, New York, NY 10010

Editor: Scott Waldman
Book Design: Michael DeLisio
Photo Researcher: Rebecca Anguin-Cohen

Photo Credits: Cover (left), p. 30 © Underwood & Underwood/Corbis; cover (right) illustr.
© Debra Wainwright/The Rosen Publishing Group; title page, p. 6 © Bettman/Corbis; p.10 cou
of Northfield Historical Society, Northfield, MN; pp.14,18, 29 courtesy of Missouri State Arch
p. 22 © Corbis; p. 31 Library of Congress Prints and Photographs Division, HABS,MO,11-SA
9-1; p. 32 Library of Congress Geography and Map Division`

First Edition

Library of Congress Cataloging-in-Publication Data

Randolph, Ryan P.
     A bank robber's end : the death of Jesse James / Ryan Randolph.
     p. cm. — (Great moments in American history)
     Summary: An account of the life and death of one of the Wild West's most
     famous outlaws, Jesse James.
     ISBN 0-8239-4359-3 (lib. bdg.)
     1. James, Jesse, 1847-1882—Juvenile literature. 2. James, Jesse,
     1847-1882—Death and burial—Juvenile literature. 3. Outlaws—West
     (U.S.)—Biography—Juvenile literature. 4. West
     (U.S.)—Biography—Juvenile literature. [1. James, Jesse, 1847-1882. 2.
     Robbers and outlaws. 3. Frontier and pioneer life—West (U.S.) 4. West
     (U.S.)—History—1860-1890.] I. Title. II. Series.

     F594.J27R36 2003
                                                        2003003921

Manufactured in the United States of America

Contents

Preface

Jesse James was one of America's most famous outlaws. He was born on September 14, 1847, in Clay County, Missouri. For most of James's life he was in a gang that robbed banks, railroads, and people. The James gang wasn't afraid to use their guns when necessary. Jesse James's cold, clear blue eyes stared down the barrel of a gun at many men.

When Jesse was a boy, Missouri allowed slavery. Jesse James's mother, Zerelda, owned slaves. When the American Civil War was fought between 1861 and 1865, people in Missouri had opposing ideas about slavery. Some agreed with the Northern states, believing that slavery should not be allowed. Others agreed with the Southern states, believing that slavery should be allowed.

Jesse and his brother Frank James joined others in Missouri who fought for the South. They were

known as bushwhackers. These fighters battled their Missouri neighbors who were on the side of the North. They would often steal horses, saddles, money, and guns during their fights.

After the Civil War ended, Jesse and Frank James were still part of the gang of bush-whackers. They continued to rob and kill people who supported the North. Many news-papers that supported the South also supported the bushwhackers. These newspapers claimed that Jesse James and his gang were fighting back because they had been driven from their homes by the Northern armies.

Other newspapers spoke out against Jesse and his gang. Rewards were offered for their capture. Many people even wanted to see Jesse James dead. For many years, he seemed unstop-pable. He always got away—until the morning of April 4, 1882....

For sixteen years, from 1866 to 1882, Frank James (center) and Jesse James (right), were feared throughout the West. Their first bank robbery was in Liberty, Missouri, on February 13, 1866. In that robbery of the Clay County Savings Bank, the brothers stole $72,000.

Chapter One

THE DEATH OF
A BANK ROBBER

The morning of April 4, 1882, started normally enough for the James family. Jesse's family lived in a small, white house in the town of St. Joseph, Missouri. St. Joseph was a small town that was growing bigger. It was located on the Missouri River. Many people worked on ships and steamboats that came in and out of the docks. People also earned money on the railroad lines that ran through town.

Maybe you're wondering how I know all this. Well, I'm Frank James, Jesse's brother. I'd like to tell you more about the death of Jesse James.

Jesse's wife, Zee, was in the kitchen with their two children, Jesse Edward James Jr. and Mary James. They were helping their mom prepare lunch.

"I'm glad Pa is here for lunch today," Jesse Jr. said.

He and his sister liked it when their father was at home. Jesse Sr. often left his family for days at a time. Jesse Jr. and Mary did not know where their dad went.

Out in the living room, Jesse and Charlie and Bob Ford were planning a bank robbery. Jesse and the Ford brothers planned to ride their horses to Platte City, Missouri, to rob the bank the next day.

CRACK!

Zee ran out of the kitchen when she heard the gunshot.

"The gun went off by accident!" yelled Charlie Ford as he and his brother Bob ran away from Jesse's home.

"Looks like it went off on purpose!" Zee screamed in anger.

In the living room, Jesse James lay dead on the floor. Bob Ford had just shot him in the head.

Police, reporters, and neighbors soon crowded into the house. It was hard for them to believe that the dead man was Jesse James. No one had been able to capture Jesse. Most people thought he would be killed in a gunfight or during a robbery. Instead, he was shot in his own home. Zee and her confused children gathered around his body. They were surrounded by many strangers who wanted to see the dead outlaw.

Jesse had been an outlaw for over fifteen years. In Missouri, he had settled down for a little while and thought about making an honest living. He put his house under the fake name Thomas Howard to protect himself and his family. I guess it's hard for some people to escape their past, though. Jesse wanted to rob another bank to make sure he and his family had plenty of money. Who knows if it really would have been his last robbery, but it was the one that got him killed.

This picture shows how the Northfield bank looked when Jesse James robbed it in 1876. The safe is through the large door in the upper right corner. Of the eight gang members involved in the robbery, only the James brothers escaped death or capture.

Chapter Two

TROUBLE IN NORTHFIELD

*J*esse and I started our gang after the Civil War ended. We still looked at people who had sided with the Northern states as enemies. In the early days of the James gang, Jesse and I gave people a lot to talk about. We weren't afraid to rob even the biggest banks. We pulled off many big robberies. Our fame grew. Most of the time everyone in the gang got away with it. We felt pretty lucky. The only problem was that we couldn't be lucky forever. One day in Northfield, Minnesota, our luck failed us.

When we rode into Northfield on April 7, 1876, our gang included our cousins, Cole, Bob, and Jim Younger. There were others, too.

Since the farmers in the western part of Minnesota had a poor crop harvest that year, we decided not to rob their banks. Instead, we went to the eastern part of the state.

Jesse and I went into the bank and drew our guns on one of the bank tellers. Outside, two of our men guarded the door. Soon, things started going badly for us. A man outside saw what we were doing and ran to get help to stop us. Meanwhile, inside the bank, we couldn't get into the safe. No one would tell us where the cash drawer was. So we threatened to kill a teller. Then things got really bad.

CRACK! CRACK! CRACK!

People had come out from all over town to shoot at us. Somebody in our gang shot the bank teller. We ran out of the bank and shot right back at the people on the street. It didn't take long for us to decide we'd had enough.

BOOM!

Just then one of our gang was lifted off of his horse when a bullet hit him in his chest.

Another man was shot in the face. Jesse and I grabbed the nearest horses. Along with the rest of the gang, we shot our way out of town.

We rode across Minnesota for a few weeks. People from all over the state had heard about our robbery. Many people were trying to capture us because there was a $2,500 reward offered to the person who could stop us. We figured we could travel faster if we split up. My brother and I rode off in one direction. The Younger brothers and the rest of the gang rode off in another.

Jesse and I traveled day and night and finally made it out of the state. The Younger brothers weren't so lucky, though. They were caught a few days after we split up.

"The Northfield bank robbery was a big mistake," Jesse told me years later. He never told this to anybody else. I only wish he had said it right after the robbery. Maybe people would have been able to forget about him. Then he'd still be alive today.

Jesse James started robbing people as a teenager and never changed his ways until his death.

Chapter Three

THE NEW JAMES GANG

After the robbery in Northfield, Jesse and I decided to settle in Tennessee. Of course, we used fake names when finding a house. We got settled for a while. For the first time in a long while, Jesse and I were no longer robbing and stealing.

"I love my family," Jesse would always say, but he could never stay in one place for very long. Jesse only settled for three years. He was itching to go back on the outlaw trail. Since he was a teenager, Jesse had lived like an outlaw. He didn't know how to live like other people. I told Jesse I wanted to stay in Tennessee to take care of my family. So Jesse left his family and went to Missouri to form a new gang. It was hard for Jesse to trust many people because there was a large reward for his capture.

Jesse formed a new gang with another cousin, Wood Hite. Jesse felt that Hite was one of the few people he could trust. Ed Miller, Dick Liddil, and Bill Ryan were some of the men in his new gang. Like Jesse and I, these men were all outlaws in Missouri.

On October 8, 1879, Jesse and his new gang rode to a train stop in Glendale, Missouri. They took the people there as prisoners. Jesse and another man moved a boulder onto the track so the train would have to stop. When the next train stopped at the station, Jesse and his gang jumped on board and pulled out their guns.

"Everyone get down!" Jesse shouted.

All the passengers laid down on the floor. But Jesse wasn't interested in their money. He knew that one of the cars had a safe with a lot of money in it. Jesse threatened to shoot one of the railroad employees if he did not turn over the keys to the safe. Once they opened the safe, two of the gang quickly stuffed all the money

into a sack. Then, as quickly as they had come, Jesse and his gang disappeared. Altogether, they had made off with about $6,000.

After that success, Jesse and his gang pulled off a lot of robberies over the next three years. Ed Miller introduced Jesse to Bob and Charlie Ford and they joined the gang. I helped out a few times as well. Things had changed, though.

"It's not like the old days," Jesse told me late one night. "I spend more time watching my back than I do robbing."

Jesse was right. Things had changed for the worse. One night he and Ed Miller got into an argument. Ed shot Jesse's hat off his head. Jesse shot back. But he didn't miss. Ed crumpled to ground. He was dead. Never had there been fighting like that in the James gang. For Jesse, the shooting of Ed Miller would later come back to haunt him.

Missouri Governor Thomas Crittendon could not capture Jesse for many years. Crittendon's luck changed, however, when he offered Bob Ford $10,000 for each of the James brothers.

Chapter Four

A DEAL GOES DOWN

*I*n March 1881, Jesse, Bill Ryan, and Wood Hite planned to hold up a man at gunpoint in Muscle Shoals, Alabama. Jesse knew the man would have money. The man was in charge of paying people in the area who worked for the government. They followed the man as he rode away from town. When he was alone they surrounded him and pulled out their guns.

"Give us the money, now!" Jesse yelled as he looked down the barrel of his gun. The man quickly turned over the bags of gold, silver, coins, and paper money he had on him.

"Search him," Jesse ordered Hite. They found another fifty dollars in paper money in the man's pocket.

"Does this money belong to you or the government?" asked Jesse.

"It is my money," replied the man.

"Give him back his money. We only steal from the government," said Jesse. "Let's ride."

Once again, Jesse and his gang got away without being caught. Jesse went back to his family in Tennessee. Shortly after the men split up, Bill Ryan got into trouble one night and was arrested. When Jesse and I read the news in the paper the next day, it worried us greatly. Bill Ryan might let people know where we were living if it meant that he would be let out of jail. That night we packed up all of our belongings. Then we took our families to Missouri.

Jesse went right back to being an outlaw. The governor of Missouri, Thomas Crittenden, badly wanted to catch Jesse and me. Governor Crittenden and the companies that had lost money during our robberies put up a reward of $10,000 to the person who could put the James brothers behind bars.

"I can't believe we're worth so much Frank," Jesse told me. I said it made me nervous.

"Me too," he replied. "That much money could turn a friend into an enemy." Unfortunately, he was right—dead right.

What we didn't know was that our old friends, Bob and Charlie Ford, were already planning to turn us in. A few weeks before, Bob had shot Wood Hite dead in an argument. The Ford brothers felt that they had repaid Jesse for killing their friend Ed Miller. Still, they were scared of what Jesse would do to them once he found out that Bob had killed his cousin.

The Ford brothers went straight to the man who most wanted to see my brother and me behind bars. On January 13, 1882, Bob Ford met with Governor Crittenden. They made a deal. Charlie and Bob Ford would not be arrested for their crimes. They would also get the reward money. All they had to do was bring in Jesse and I—dead or alive.

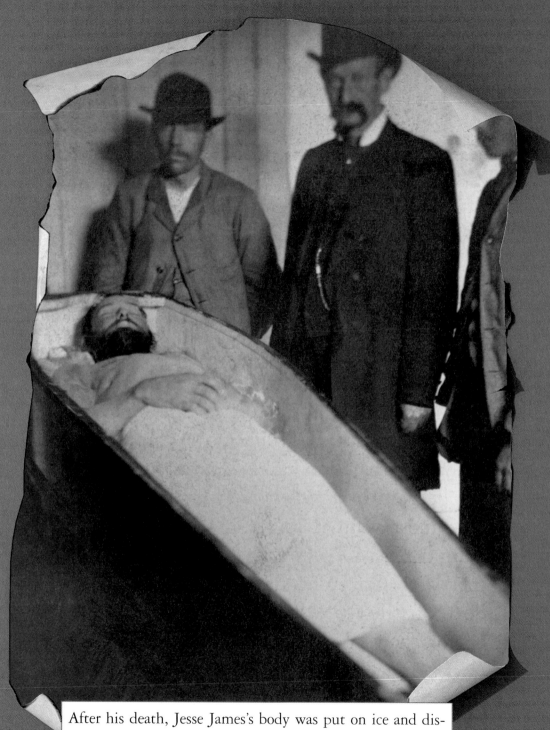

After his death, Jesse James's body was put on ice and displayed in a funeral parlor. The scars on his right side are from a Civil War injury.

Chapter Five

COWARDS OR HEROES?

*J*esse and I had no idea that Charlie and Bob Ford had made an agreement with the governor to get us. Most of our old gang was gone. Ed Miller and Wood Hite were dead. Bill Ryan was in jail. I was trying to lay low while in Missouri.

Jesse knew there was a large reward for his capture. But he cared more about getting the banks' money than he did the law. He planned to rob a bank in Platte City, Missouri, with the Ford brothers.

A couple of days before the Platte City robbery was supposed to happen, Jesse told the Ford brothers something strange.

"So many people want to get that reward money for me," he said. "I might get caught soon. Before I go down though, I'm going to shake up this country once or twice more."

Bob and Charlie knew that Jesse was quicker with his guns than they were with theirs. What would happen if Jesse found out what they were planning? It was better not to think about it. The Fords could only hope that they would catch Jesse without his guns sometime soon.

On April 4, the day before the planned robbery, the Fords arrived at Jesse's house early in the morning. Jesse and Charlie went out to the barn to feed the horses. Even though it was only April, it was a hot day. When they went back into the house, Jesse took off his coat. His pistols were strapped around his chest.

"I better take off these pistols," said Jesse. "My neighbors might think it was strange if I wore guns just to work in the yard."

Bob and Charlie Ford looked at each other as Jesse took off his guns. Neither said a word.

"How did this picture get so crooked?" said Jesse as he turned toward the wall. He pulled over a chair and stood on it to adjust the picture. His back was turned to the Fords.

Charlie nodded to Bob. The brothers pulled out their pistols.

Click. Click.

They cocked their guns to fire. Bob was faster and shot first. He shot Jesse in the back of the head just as he was turning around. Jesse fell off the chair and hit the floor with a loud thud.

The Fords ran to the telegraph office to tell the police. Then they went back to the murder site. The Fords bragged that they had killed Jesse James.

But their plan backfired. The Ford brothers were arrested for murder. Some newspapers said they were cowards for shooting Jesse in the back. Other newspapers said the Ford brothers were heroes. Still others did not want the Fords to have the reward money. The reward was for the *capture* of Jesse James these newspapers said. It was not for his *murder,* they said. At that time, not many people knew about the secret deal that the Fords had made with Governor Crittendon.

Of course, I've always thought the Fords were cowards for shooting Jesse in the back. But it was the life Jesse chose to lead. He had killed many people over the years. He had robbed even more. In the last year of his life, Jesse lived in fear that someone was going to do him in. It finally happened.

In the end, the governor got the Ford brothers out of jail. Charlie Ford killed himself in 1884, just two years after he helped kill Jesse. Bob Ford was shot and killed in Colorado in 1892.

Me? I'm still alive. It is 1910. I have outlived the Fords and most of my family. By 1885, I was cleared of all the crimes I was charged with over the years. Since then, I've made my living as a farmer. Mostly, I don't think about the old days anymore. But every once and a while, I like to tell stories about America's greatest outlaw—the famous Jesse James—and how he met his end.

GLOSSARY

bushwhackers (BUSH-wak-uhrs) a group of outlaws that fought for the South in the Civil War

Civil War (SIV-il WOR) the U.S. war between the Confederacy, or Southern states, and the Union, or Northern states, that lasted from 1861-1865

cowards (KOU-urdz) people who are easily scared and run away from frightening situations

governor (GUHV-urn-ur) the person who governs a state

government (GUHV-urn-muhnt) the people who rule or govern a country

outlaw (OUT-law) a criminal, especially one who is running away from the law

pistols (PISS-tuhlz) small guns designed to be held in the hand

surrounded (suh-ROUND-ehd) to have something on every side of something else

telegraph (TEL-uh-graf) a device or system for sending messages over long distances using a code of electrical signals sent by wire or radio

Primary Sources

Studying old photographs, drawings, and other sources can help us draw conclusions about Jesse James. Posters such as the one on page 30 were put in towns where James might have been hiding. There weren't many photographs of Jesse James at the time so the poster does not have a picture of him. People didn't know what he looked like. After looking at the poster, it is possible to understand how Jesse James was able to get away with so many crimes.

The drawing on page 32 shows the town of Saint Joseph, Missouri, as it looked in the late 1800s. The train and riverboats show us how people traveled. There are also more houses near the river's edge than anywhere else in town. This is because most people worked in that area. Illustrations like this help us compare and contrast how people lived at the time to the way they live now. Studying sources from the past helps us find the clues to learn about people, places, and events from many years ago.

Mary James and Jesse Edwards James Jr. did not know who their father really was until after he died. Jesse Jr. later became a respected lawyer.

The more trains and banks the James brothers robbed, the higher the reward offered for them was. When Jesse was shot, he was worth $10,000. This is an old Wanted poster. Wanted posters were put up in towns as a way to catch outlaws.

Jesse James was shot in this house. When people started coming to see the house after his death, it was moved to a new location in Missouri and used as a museum.

This is how Saint Joseph, Missouri, looked in the late 1800s, when James was living there. Notice the trains and riverboats in the picture. Many people in town worked for the railroads or on boats.